As seen on
The RBL FESTIVAL OF REMEMBRANCE

ALIVE
WITH
POPPIES

TOMOS ROBERTS
Illustrated by SHARON RENTTA

■SCHOLASTIC

Alive with poppies for Remembrance,
We all fall silent at the hour.
But what's the meaning of this moment?
Why do so many wear a flower?

Hardly more than a hundred years ago,
Came a call impossible to ignore.

A global conflict was emerging,
And too, the rumblings of war.

People then lived lives just like ours,
They played, they worked, they chased their dreams.

Although the life they knew was changing,
The world unravelled at its seams.

They were sent to unfamiliar countries,
With still so much to live and learn,
They waved goodbye to those who loved them
And knew they may never return.

It wasn't that they wished for conflict.
They kept up hope that it would cease.
They put their bodies in that danger,
So that in time we'd live in peace.

So many young and brave and hopeful,
Fought for a world they'd never know.
And fields, once green, now stained with blood,
Became a place where poppies grow.

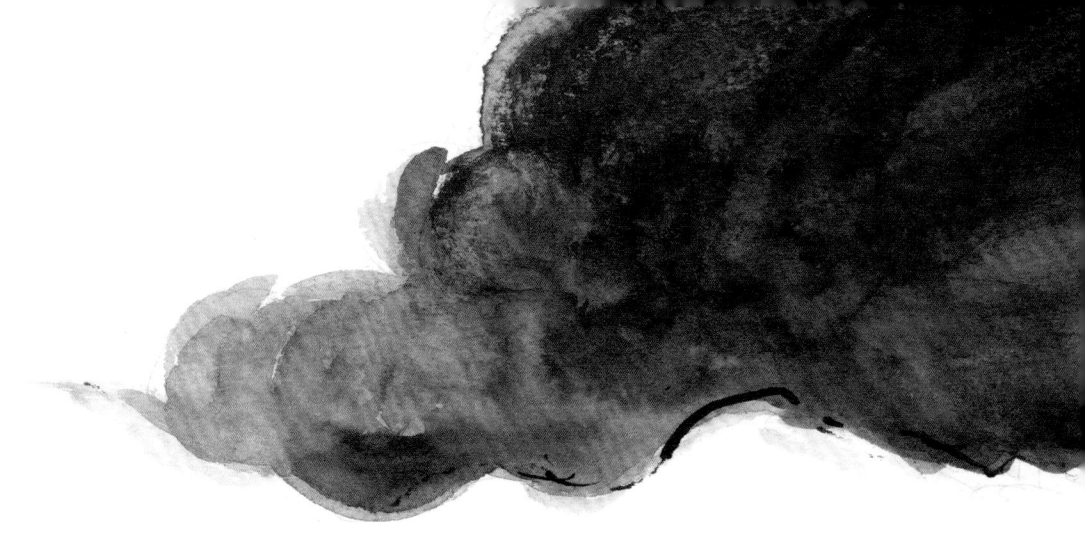

Neither you nor I can truly know
How they endured the hand they were dealt.
But on this day, and in this moment,
We can try to imagine how they felt.

There was a soldier who was also a poet,
In Flanders Fields, 1916.
And he penned a poem rich and haunting
About the poppies he had seen.

And through the symbol of that flower,
Those who survived could dare to hope.
And would commemorate the fallen,
Now through the stories that they spoke.

It was a poppy for their contribution,
Since every human life is equal.
A reminder that the war to end all wars
Must never have a sequel.

But barely more than two decades later,
Once again, the shrapnel fell.

And once again brave souls would go to fight,
To face their last farewell.

But they kept believing, through the darkness,
That in their time the day would come.
The day the fight that they endured
Would, like all things, one day be done.

From then till now we've still known conflict,
And we've still known loss of life.
And still, so many men and women
Have made the utmost sacrifice.

Because the call never goes unanswered,
Any time our values meet with a threat.
And in light of that, we still mark silence,
As we give thanks and pay respect.

That's why today we wear a poppy!
For battles past to modern day.
And while courage guides our hearts and minds,
That can never slip away.

It is why our hope must never falter.
It is why I even dare to dream
That a hundred years and more from now,
Children will still know what it means.

And on their path to peace and progress,
Each one of them will always know

The story of the way that path was built,
And the ones who made it so.

So on this day, alive with poppies –
With petals red and leaves of green,
A symbol echoing a sacrifice,
A memory guarding what it means,

We share this moment for Remembrance.
We remember all who came before.
As through remembrance we honour them,
And hold that hope, forevermore.

Author's Note

I once asked my grandmother, born in 1929 in the Welsh valleys, about her memories of the Second World War. She recalled a night aged twelve when her father took her to the pictures, and as they left, she could see the distant bombs falling on Swansea, lighting up the night sky. Last year, my big sister gave birth to a lovely little boy named Felix, who spent his first Christmas in the arms of his adoring great grandmother before her passing in early 2024.

Through this story of Remembrance, my hope is to express gratitude to all who lived lives of service and sacrifice, while holding onto hope that future generations need not endure the same.

I dedicate this book to Catherine Ann Francis and Felix Rhys Francis King.

Published in the UK by Scholastic, 2024
1 London Bridge, London, SE1 9BG
Scholastic Ireland, 89E Lagan Road, Dublin Industrial Estate, Glasnevin, Dublin, D11 HP5F

SCHOLASTIC and associated logos are trademarks and/or registered trademarks of Scholastic Inc.

First published in the UK by Scholastic, 2024
Text © Author name, Tomos Roberts

Illustrations © Illustrator name, Sharon Rentta

The right of Tomos Roberts and Sharon Rentta to be identified as the author and illustrator of this work has been asserted by them under the Copyright, Designs and Patents Act 1988.

ISBN 978 07023 3339 2

A CIP catalogue record for this book is available from the British Library.
All rights reserved.

This book is sold subject to the condition that it shall not, by way of trade or otherwise, be lent, hired out or otherwise circulated in any form of binding or cover other than that in which it is published. No part of this publication may be reproduced, stored in a retrieval system, or transmitted in any form or by any other means (electronic, mechanical, photocopying, recording or otherwise) without prior written permission of Scholastic Limited.

Printed in China

Paper made from wood grown in sustainable forests and other controlled sources.

1 3 5 7 9 10 8 6 4 2

This is a work of fiction. Names, characters, places, incidents and dialogues are products of the author's imagination or are used fictitiously. Any resemblance to actual people, living or dead, events or locales is entirely coincidental.

www.scholastic.co.uk